Mastering LM Studio to Create AI Agents Locally

Master the Art of Local AI Development with LM Studio: A Comprehensive Guide to Building, Optimizing, and Integrating AI Agents

CONTENTS :

- Recommended configurations for optimal performance

2.2 Downloading and Installing LM Studio

- Step-by-step guide for Windows, macOS, and Linux
- Troubleshooting installation issues

2.3 Setting Up Your Environment

- Configuration settings
- Installing necessary dependencies
- Verifying the installation

Chapter 3: Choosing and Downloading AI Models

3.1 Understanding AI Models in LM Studio

- Supported model architectures (DeepSeek, LLaMA, Mistral, etc.)
- Choosing the right model for your AI agent

3.2 Downloading AI Models

- Where to find models
- How to download and import models into LM Studio

3.3 Optimizing Model Performance

- Managing system resources
- Using quantized models for efficiency

Chapter 4: Developing an AI Agent Locally

4.1 Setting Up Your AI Agent

- Selecting the base model
- Configuring prompts and responses

4.2 Training and Fine-Tuning Models

- Methods for fine-tuning
- Using local datasets for training
- Adjusting hyperparameters for better performance

4.3 Implementing Custom Behaviors

- Creating personality and context awareness
- Using prompt engineering techniques
- Setting up multi-turn conversation memory

Chapter 5: Integrating AI Agents into Applications

5.1 Connecting LM Studio with APIs

- API integration basics
- Using Python and JavaScript for interaction

5.2 Building a Chatbot with LM Studio

- Frameworks for chatbot development
- Example code snippets for chatbot integration

5.3 Enhancing Functionality with Plugins and Extensions

- Adding voice support
- Connecting with databases and automation tools

Chapter 6: Optimizing and Troubleshooting

6.1 Performance Optimization

- Reducing latency and improving response times
- Using GPU acceleration

6.2 Common Issues and Fixes

- Model loading errors
- Memory and performance troubleshooting
- Compatibility issues

6.3 Best Practices for Running AI Locally

- Security considerations
- Data privacy measures
- Keeping models updated

Chapter 7: Future of Local AI Agents

7.1 Emerging Trends in Local AI Development

- Advances in lightweight models
- Future improvements in LM Studio

7.2 Expanding AI Agent Capabilities

- Multimodal AI (text, image, audio processing)
- Local AI in edge computing and IoT

Conclusion

Mastering LM Studio to Create AI Agents Locally

Master the Art of Local AI Development with LM Studio: A Comprehensive Guide to Building, Optimizing, and Integrating AI Agents

Introduction

In today's rapidly evolving world of artificial intelligence, the ability to develop and deploy AI models locally offers numerous advantages, particularly when it comes to privacy, control, and efficiency. LM Studio is a powerful tool designed for those who wish to harness the potential of machine learning models without relying on cloud-based solutions. This powerful platform enables developers to build, train, and deploy AI agents locally, allowing them to take full control over their models, datasets, and computational resources. By offering a user-friendly interface and seamless integration with various AI frameworks, LM Studio simplifies the complex process of AI agent development, making it accessible for both beginners and experienced developers.

One of the standout benefits of running AI models locally is enhanced privacy. Unlike cloud-based AI services that store sensitive data on external servers, local AI development ensures that your data remains within your own infrastructure. This is especially critical when handling confidential information or when working in industries that require strict data governance standards. Running AI models locally also allows for better optimization and faster execution times since the models can be fine-tuned to work with the specific hardware you're using, rather than being dependent on a shared cloud infrastructure.

LM Studio, with its intuitive tools and flexible capabilities, is an ideal choice for AI agent development. Whether you are building a chatbot, a recommendation system, or a more complex machine learning agent, LM Studio streamlines the entire process from data preparation to deployment. The local execution of models means that developers can experiment and iterate without the constraints often associated with cloud-based AI services, such as latency and network issues. Moreover, LM Studio supports a variety of machine learning frameworks, making it compatible with a wide range of algorithms and technologies, ensuring that developers have the flexibility they need to create sophisticated AI solutions tailored to their specific use cases.

This guide will explore the full potential of LM Studio and how you can leverage its features to develop AI agents that operate entirely within your local environment. From setting up the software to mastering advanced development techniques, you'll gain a comprehensive understanding of how to harness the power of LM Studio to create robust, efficient, and secure AI agents. Whether you're just starting your journey into AI or you're looking to deepen your expertise, mastering LM Studio opens up a world of possibilities for local AI development.

Chapter 1: Understanding LM Studio

1.1 What is LM Studio?

Definition and Purpose

LM Studio is a robust, user-friendly platform designed for the development, training, and deployment of machine learning models locally. It is an integrated development environment (IDE) that allows developers to work with AI models directly on their own hardware, eliminating the need for external cloud resources. This powerful tool is ideal for those who want to build and run AI applications—ranging from simple agents to complex systems—without the constraints and overheads of cloud-based AI services.

The primary purpose of LM Studio is to streamline the AI development process, providing a seamless workflow that takes you from data processing and model training to deployment. Whether you're working on natural language processing, computer vision, or any other machine learning discipline, LM Studio offers the necessary features to handle all aspects of AI agent development. With built-in support for popular AI frameworks, it allows developers to design, test, and optimize models in a way that suits their specific needs and local environment.

Key Features and Advantages

LM Studio is designed with both simplicity and flexibility in mind. Some of its key features include:

- **Local Execution**: The ability to run AI models on your own hardware without the need for an internet connection or reliance on cloud services. This means that all processing and computations happen on your local machine, which can be particularly useful for privacy and speed.
- **Support for Popular AI Frameworks**: LM Studio is compatible with widely-used machine learning libraries and frameworks such as TensorFlow, PyTorch, and Keras. This makes it easy to implement state-of-the-art models and algorithms.
- **Intuitive User Interface**: The platform provides a clean, intuitive interface that simplifies the development process. From data pre-processing to model training, testing, and deployment, everything can be managed from one central hub.
- **Customization and Extendability**: LM Studio allows users to extend its functionality through custom plugins, scripts, and integrations. This makes it an excellent choice for developers who want to create highly specialized AI applications.
- **Efficiency and Optimization**: With LM Studio, developers can take advantage of their own computational resources, optimizing models based on the specific hardware they have, such as GPUs or CPUs, for faster execution.

1.2 Why Use LM Studio for AI Agents?

Offline AI Model Execution

One of the primary reasons to use LM Studio for AI agents is the ability to execute models offline. In a world where data privacy and security are increasingly important, having the option to run AI models locally ensures that your sensitive data remains within your control. Instead of sending your data to external cloud servers, you can store and process everything on your own machine, providing greater control over your information and mitigating risks associated with data leaks or breaches. Moreover, working offline also eliminates the dependency on an internet connection, allowing you to continue your development even in environments with limited or no connectivity.

Privacy and Security Benefits

Privacy and security are major concerns for many AI applications. With LM Studio, all data processing and model execution remain on your own hardware, which means you have full control over who accesses the data and how it's handled. Unlike cloud-based solutions, which may require you to upload data to third-party servers, LM Studio ensures that your sensitive information is kept private. For organizations dealing with confidential data or industries that require strict regulatory compliance (such as healthcare or finance), using LM Studio to build and deploy AI models locally helps mitigate the risk of data exposure.

No Reliance on Cloud Services

By using LM Studio, you eliminate the need to rely on external cloud services for AI model execution. Cloud-based services, while convenient, can be costly and come with limitations such as service outages, latency issues, and data transfer fees. LM Studio allows you to bypass these challenges by enabling local execution of models, saving you both time and money. Additionally, by running AI models locally, you avoid the complexities of managing cloud subscriptions and can optimize your development process without external dependencies.

Customization and Flexibility

LM Studio provides unparalleled customization and flexibility, making it an ideal choice for developers who need to tailor their AI agents to specific requirements. The platform's open architecture allows you to fine-tune and adapt its features to fit your unique use cases. Whether you're integrating different machine learning models, experimenting with new algorithms, or adjusting hyperparameters to achieve optimal performance, LM Studio gives you the freedom to modify every aspect of your development workflow. This level of flexibility is often limited in cloud-based AI platforms, where users must adhere to predefined services and configurations.

By offering these advantages, LM Studio empowers developers to create high-performance AI agents with full control over the development, execution, and optimization processes. Whether you're building simple models or complex, multi-faceted AI systems, LM Studio's offline capabilities, privacy benefits, and customization options make it the ideal choice for local AI agent development.

Chapter 2: Installing and Setting Up LM Studio

2.1 System Requirements

Hardware and Software Prerequisites

Before installing LM Studio, it's essential to ensure that your system meets the necessary hardware and software requirements. LM Studio is designed to work efficiently on a wide range of systems, but meeting the minimum prerequisites will help you get the best performance out of the platform.

Hardware Requirements:

- **Processor**: A multi-core CPU (Intel Core i5 or equivalent minimum). For optimal performance, a more powerful processor such as an Intel i7 or AMD Ryzen 7 is recommended.
- **Memory (RAM)**: At least 8 GB of RAM (16 GB or more recommended for handling large models and datasets).
- **Storage**: A solid-state drive (SSD) with a minimum of 10 GB of free space for installation and development purposes. More space may be required for larger datasets and model storage.

- **Graphics Card (Optional but Recommended)**: For those working with deep learning models, a dedicated GPU (NVIDIA with CUDA support) will significantly speed up training and inference times.

Software Requirements:

- **Operating System**: LM Studio supports the following operating systems:
  - **Windows 10 (64-bit) or later**
  - **macOS 10.15 (Catalina) or later**
  - **Linux (Ubuntu 20.04 or later)**
- **Python**: Version 3.7 or higher (most ML libraries are built for Python 3+).
- **Dependencies**: LM Studio may require some libraries like TensorFlow, PyTorch, or other frameworks, depending on your use case.

Recommended Configurations for Optimal Performance

To ensure that LM Studio runs at its best, consider these recommendations:

- **CPU**: A modern multi-core processor (Intel Core i7 or AMD Ryzen 7) will provide faster execution for complex AI models.
- **Memory (RAM)**: 16 GB of RAM or more will prevent slowdowns when working with large datasets or running resource-heavy models.

- **Storage**: Use an SSD with at least 100 GB of available space, especially for AI projects that involve large data files and model checkpoints.
- **GPU**: A dedicated GPU with at least 4 GB of VRAM (NVIDIA GTX 1660 Ti or better) will significantly boost training and inference speeds, particularly for deep learning tasks.

2.2 Downloading and Installing LM Studio

Step-by-Step Guide for Windows, macOS, and Linux

Here's a simple guide to downloading and installing LM Studio on different operating systems:

For Windows:

1. Visit the official LM Studio website and navigate to the **Download** page.
2. Select the Windows version of LM Studio (ensure it's compatible with your system, either 32-bit or 64-bit).
3. Download the installer file (usually a .exe file).
4. Once downloaded, double-click the installer to begin the installation process.
5. Follow the on-screen prompts, accept the license agreement, and choose the installation location.
6. Click **Install** and wait for the process to complete.
7. Once installed, you can launch LM Studio from the Start Menu or Desktop shortcut.

For macOS:

1. Visit the official LM Studio website and navigate to the **Download** page.
2. Download the macOS version of LM Studio.
3. Open the downloaded `.dmg` file.
4. Drag and drop the LM Studio icon into the **Applications** folder.
5. Once installation is complete, you can launch LM Studio from the Applications folder or Launchpad.

For Linux (Ubuntu):

1. Visit the LM Studio website and download the Linux version (usually provided as a `.tar.gz` or `.deb` file).
2. For `.deb` files:
   - Open a terminal and navigate to the directory where the file was downloaded.
   - Install the package using the following command:
   - `sudo dpkg -i lm-studio-version.deb`
3. For `.tar.gz` files:
   - Extract the downloaded file using:
   - `tar -xzvf lm-studio-version.tar.gz`
   - Follow the README instructions in the extracted folder to complete installation.
4. After installation, you can launch LM Studio from your Applications menu or by running the appropriate command from the terminal.

Troubleshooting Installation Issues

If you encounter any issues during installation, consider the following solutions:

- **Windows**: If you see an error related to missing DLL files, ensure your system has the necessary Visual C++ Redistributable packages installed. These can be downloaded from Microsoft's website.
- **macOS**: If you can't open LM Studio after installation, check your security preferences to ensure apps from identified developers are allowed. Go to **System Preferences > Security & Privacy**, and click **Open Anyway** if needed.
- **Linux**: If dependencies are missing after installation, try running:
- `sudo apt-get install -f`

This command will automatically install any missing dependencies for LM Studio.

2.3 Setting Up Your Environment

Configuration Settings

Once LM Studio is installed, the next step is to configure it for your development needs. Launch LM Studio and navigate to the **Settings** or **Preferences** menu. Here, you can customize various aspects of your development environment, such as:

- **Project Directory**: Choose the default folder where your AI projects will be saved.
- **Python Interpreter**: Select the Python version and environment you want to use (e.g., a virtual environment or the system Python).
- **GPU/CPU Settings**: If you have a compatible GPU, enable GPU acceleration for faster model training and inference.

Installing Necessary Dependencies

LM Studio may require additional dependencies depending on your specific project. To install the required libraries and tools:

1. Open the **Terminal** or **Command Prompt** from within LM Studio.
2. Use the following commands to install the necessary dependencies:
   - For **TensorFlow** (CPU version):
   - `pip install tensorflow`
   - For **PyTorch** (CPU version):
   - `pip install torch`
   - For **Keras**:
   - `pip install keras`
3. If you plan to use GPU acceleration, you may need to install GPU-specific versions of these libraries. Follow the instructions on the respective framework's website for installing GPU-accelerated versions.

Verifying the Installation

After setting up LM Studio and installing the necessary dependencies, it's important to verify that everything is working correctly:

1. Open LM Studio and create a new project.
2. Import a sample dataset or model (you can use sample datasets provided within the LM Studio platform).
3. Try running a basic model (e.g., a simple linear regression or a small neural network) to test if everything is functioning as expected.
4. If the model runs without issues and displays results, the installation and environment setup are complete.

By following these steps, you'll have LM Studio installed and configured on your system, ready to start building AI agents locally!

Chapter 3: Choosing and Downloading AI Models

3.1 Understanding AI Models in LM Studio

Supported Model Architectures (DeepSeek, LLaMA, Mistral, etc.)

LM Studio supports a range of powerful AI model architectures, each suited to different tasks and applications. These models include cutting-edge frameworks like DeepSeek, LLaMA, and Mistral, which have distinct strengths for various AI projects. Here's a brief overview of some popular model architectures you can use in LM Studio:

- **DeepSeek**: Designed primarily for advanced natural language processing (NLP) tasks, DeepSeek excels at handling large language models (LLMs) and providing high-level semantic understanding of text. It's particularly effective for tasks like text generation, question answering, and summarization.
- **LLaMA (Large Language Model Meta AI)**: Developed by Meta (formerly Facebook), LLaMA is a series of large, dense transformer-based models designed for general-purpose language understanding. These models are optimized for a wide variety of NLP tasks, from simple text classification to more complex reasoning and generation tasks. LLaMA is well-known for being

highly efficient at scale, and it works well for both research and commercial applications.

- **Mistral**: Mistral is an open-source, dense, autoregressive model focused on being both lightweight and powerful. It's designed for various applications, including NLP, data generation, and more. Mistral models are known for their speed and efficiency, making them ideal for real-time processing tasks.
- **Other Supported Models**: LM Studio also supports a wide variety of additional models tailored to specific domains, including computer vision, reinforcement learning, and time-series analysis. Examples include Vision Transformers (ViT) for image classification and OpenAI's GPT models for language generation.

Choosing the Right Model for Your AI Agent

Selecting the right AI model is crucial to ensuring that your AI agent functions optimally. The model you choose depends on several factors, including the task at hand, the size of the dataset, available computational resources, and the performance requirements of your AI system. Here's how you can choose the best model for your needs:

- **Task Type**: Consider the specific task your AI agent needs to perform. For example:
  - **Text-based tasks (e.g., chatbots, summarization)**: Large language models like **DeepSeek** and **LLaMA** are ideal for

NLP tasks, thanks to their ability to understand and generate human-like text.

- o **Image-based tasks (e.g., object recognition, segmentation)**: Vision models like **ViT** or **ResNet** would be more appropriate for image processing tasks.
- o **Multimodal tasks**: If your AI agent needs to process both text and images, models that combine these domains, such as CLIP (Contrastive Language–Image Pretraining), may be the best fit.

- **Computational Resources**: Some models, particularly large ones like LLaMA or GPT-3, can be computationally expensive. Consider the hardware available on your system. If you have limited resources, a lighter model like **Mistral** or **DistilBERT** may be more appropriate.
- **Performance**: Larger models typically provide more accurate results, but they also consume more memory and require longer training times. If you need a balance between performance and efficiency, look into using **quantized models** or lighter variants like **DistilBERT**, which preserve much of the performance but are more resource-efficient.

3.2 Downloading AI Models

Where to Find Models

Once you've chosen a model, the next step is to download it and prepare it for use in LM Studio. Fortunately, there are several resources where you can find pre-trained AI models for free or with minimal cost:

- **Official Model Repositories**: Popular AI frameworks like TensorFlow, PyTorch, and Hugging Face offer pre-trained models in their official repositories:
  - **Hugging Face Model Hub**: A massive collection of pre-trained models for NLP, computer vision, and other tasks. You can easily search for models based on your needs.
  - **TensorFlow Hub**: TensorFlow's official hub for machine learning models, including models for text, image, and audio processing.
  - **PyTorch Hub**: Similar to TensorFlow Hub, but specifically for PyTorch-based models.
- **Model Zoos and Community Repositories**: Various communities and open-source projects maintain model zoos where you can find cutting-edge models. Examples include the **DeepSeek** model repository or GitHub-based repositories for **LLaMA** or **Mistral**.
- **LM Studio Marketplace**: Some developers and organizations may provide additional models on the LM Studio marketplace or similar platforms. These

models are often fine-tuned and optimized for specific applications.

How to Download and Import Models into LM Studio

1. **Find the model**: Search for the model you want from any of the above-mentioned sources.
2. **Download the model**: Models are typically available in formats like `.h5` (for Keras/TensorFlow), `.pt` (for PyTorch), or `.bin` (for Hugging Face models). Make sure to download the appropriate version for your framework.
3. **Import into LM Studio**:
   - **Via GUI**: Open LM Studio and go to the **Models** section. There should be an option to **Import Model**. Select the downloaded model file and follow the prompts to import it into the platform.
   - **Via Command Line**: You can also use the terminal within LM Studio to import models:
   - `lmstudio import <path_to_model_file>`
4. **Verify the model**: Once imported, you can test the model by running a sample inference or loading it into a new project to ensure that it was correctly imported.

3.3 Optimizing Model Performance

Managing System Resources

When working with large AI models, managing system resources is essential to ensure smooth execution and optimal performance. Here are a few tips to optimize resource usage:

- **Use GPUs**: If your system has a dedicated GPU, make sure to enable GPU acceleration. This will significantly speed up training and inference times for deep learning models.
- **Batch Processing**: When working with large datasets or complex models, consider using batch processing to divide tasks into smaller chunks that can be handled more easily by your system.
- **Memory Management**: Keep an eye on your system's memory usage, especially when working with large models. If you notice memory limitations, consider reducing the batch size, using smaller models, or upgrading your hardware.
- **Model Checkpoints**: Saving model checkpoints during training allows you to resume from the last successful state without losing progress, especially when you encounter system failures or long training periods.

Using Quantized Models for Efficiency

Quantization is a technique that reduces the precision of the numbers used in a model's weights and activations, resulting in a smaller model size and faster execution. Quantized models can perform almost as well as their full-precision counterparts but require less memory and computation.

Here's how you can use quantized models in LM Studio:

- **Download Quantized Versions**: Some models are available in quantized versions on model repositories. For example, Hugging Face provides many models with quantization options.
- **Convert a Model to Quantized Format**: If the model you are using doesn't come in a quantized format, you can convert it using libraries like **TensorFlow Lite** or **PyTorch Quantization**.
- **Implement Quantized Models in LM Studio**: Once you've obtained or converted a model to a quantized format, you can import it into LM Studio just like any other model and begin using it to run inference or further training tasks.

Quantized models are particularly useful for deploying AI agents in resource-constrained environments like mobile devices or edge devices, as they provide a great trade-off between performance and resource usage.

By selecting the right model, downloading it efficiently, and optimizing its performance, you can ensure that your AI agent runs smoothly and efficiently, whether on a local machine or in more specialized environments.

Chapter 4: Developing an AI Agent Locally

4.1 Setting Up Your AI Agent

Selecting the Base Model

The first step in developing your AI agent is choosing the right base model. This model will serve as the foundation for your AI agent's functionality, so selecting an appropriate one is crucial. Consider the following factors when making your choice:

- **Task Scope**: Determine the type of tasks your AI agent will perform. If your agent is meant for simple tasks like text-based question answering or customer support, a model like **DeepSeek** or **LLaMA** will suffice. For more advanced tasks, such as complex reasoning or multimodal processing, consider larger models that support these functionalities.
- **Model Size**: Larger models like **LLaMA** may provide better performance but at the cost of requiring more resources. If you have limited computational resources, you may want to consider smaller, more efficient models like **Mistral** or a quantized variant of a larger model.
- **Fine-Tuning Capability**: Some models are more adaptable for fine-tuning, which is crucial if you want to train your agent for specific use cases. **DeepSeek** and **LLaMA** support extensive fine-

tuning, which can help tailor your agent to your specific needs.

Once you've chosen the model, you can begin setting up your AI agent in LM Studio. The process involves importing the base model and configuring it to handle user inputs, process data, and provide responses.

Configuring Prompts and Responses

For your AI agent to communicate effectively, you'll need to configure prompts and define how the agent will respond. This setup involves the following steps:

1. **Designing the Conversation Flow**: Define the types of conversations your AI agent will handle. Will it be a Q&A bot, a personal assistant, or an agent designed for more complex discussions? Identify the key objectives for your agent's interactions.
2. **Creating Prompt Templates**: Create prompts that will guide the AI agent's responses. In LM Studio, you can configure these prompts by defining input parameters and the type of output you expect. For example, if you are developing a customer support agent, your prompt may look like:
3. User: "How do I reset my password?"
4. AI Agent: "To reset your password, please follow these steps..."
5. **Customizing Responses**: Fine-tune how the agent responds by adjusting the tone, style, and level of detail. Depending on your needs, you can make the

agent respond in a formal tone or a more casual, conversational style.

By tailoring the prompts and responses to your specific use case, you ensure that your AI agent communicates in the desired way, creating an engaging and effective interaction with users.

4.2 Training and Fine-Tuning Models

Methods for Fine-Tuning

Fine-tuning is the process of adapting a pre-trained model to specific tasks or domains. In LM Studio, you can fine-tune a model to make it more effective for your AI agent's needs. Here are some common methods:

- **Supervised Fine-Tuning**: This method involves training the model with labeled data, where the correct output is provided for each input. This approach helps the model adjust its internal weights to perform better on tasks similar to those in the labeled dataset.
- **Reinforcement Learning**: For tasks that require the agent to improve based on trial and error (e.g., decision-making tasks), reinforcement learning can be used to fine-tune the model. In this scenario, the agent interacts with an environment and receives feedback based on its actions, adjusting its behavior over time.

- **Transfer Learning**: This method involves taking a model pre-trained on a large dataset and fine-tuning it on a smaller, domain-specific dataset. This is ideal if you want your agent to specialize in a certain area without starting from scratch.

Using Local Datasets for Training

When training or fine-tuning your AI agent, it's essential to use datasets that are relevant to your specific use case. LM Studio allows you to import local datasets and use them for training. Here's how to get started:

1. **Prepare Your Dataset**: Format your dataset according to the task you are training for. For example, if you're training a chatbot, your dataset might consist of question-answer pairs, dialogue examples, or customer service transcripts.
2. **Import the Dataset**: LM Studio supports several formats for importing datasets, including CSV, JSON, and text files. Once the dataset is prepared, you can easily upload it into LM Studio via the **Data Importer**.
3. **Fine-Tuning Process**: After importing the dataset, you can start fine-tuning the model by running training scripts. LM Studio allows you to specify parameters such as learning rate, batch size, and epochs. This ensures that your model learns effectively from the data.

Adjusting Hyperparameters for Better Performance

Fine-tuning performance also depends on how you adjust the model's hyperparameters. These parameters control the training process and can significantly impact the outcome. Common hyperparameters include:

- **Learning Rate**: Controls how quickly the model adjusts during training. A high learning rate may lead to faster convergence but risks overshooting the optimal solution, while a lower rate results in slower training but better precision.
- **Batch Size**: Defines the number of training samples the model processes before updating its parameters. Larger batch sizes lead to faster training but require more memory, while smaller batch sizes reduce memory usage but may slow down the process.
- **Epochs**: Represents the number of times the model sees the entire dataset during training. More epochs generally improve accuracy, but training for too long can result in overfitting.

Adjusting these hyperparameters through experimentation and validation will help you achieve the best model performance for your AI agent.

4.3 Implementing Custom Behaviors

Creating Personality and Context Awareness

One of the most important aspects of developing an AI agent is giving it personality and context awareness. This helps ensure that the agent feels more human-like and can handle various scenarios in a way that aligns with its intended purpose.

- **Defining Personality**: You can define your agent's personality by configuring its tone, conversational style, and behavior patterns. For example, if you are building a support agent, you might want it to be polite and formal. On the other hand, for a chatbot designed for casual conversation, a relaxed, humorous tone might be more appropriate.
- **Context Awareness**: Context awareness allows your agent to remember past interactions and respond accordingly. For example, if a user asks a follow-up question, the agent should recall the previous conversation and provide a relevant answer. This adds a level of coherence to the interaction, making it feel more like a natural conversation.

Using Prompt Engineering Techniques

Prompt engineering is the process of designing the input prompts to guide the model toward producing the desired outputs. This can help your AI agent generate responses that align with the agent's personality and objectives. Techniques for prompt engineering include:

- **Clear Instructions**: Provide the model with explicit instructions on how to respond. For example:
  - `"You are a helpful assistant. Please provide a step-by-step guide to reset the password."`

- **Injecting Context**: Include relevant context in the prompt to help the model generate more informed responses. For instance:
  - `"User: I need to reset my password. I forgot it. Can you help?"`

Setting Up Multi-Turn Conversation Memory

For a truly interactive AI agent, it's important to implement multi-turn conversation memory. This allows the AI agent to keep track of previous user inputs and maintain continuity in the conversation. In LM Studio, you can configure memory management by storing conversation history in a session. The agent can then access this history when generating responses, ensuring that it provides contextually accurate and relevant replies.

To set up multi-turn memory:

1. **Store User Input**: After each user input, store the message and the corresponding agent response in a session history.
2. **Access Memory**: When the user asks a follow-up question, retrieve the previous interactions and use them to craft a response that acknowledges the context.
3. **Contextual Prompts**: Include the conversation history in the prompt to provide context for the current response.

By combining these strategies, your AI agent will be able to carry on multi-turn conversations and respond in a personalized, contextually aware manner.

With these techniques, you'll be well-equipped to develop an AI agent that can respond intelligently, learn over time, and provide a dynamic and engaging user experience. Whether it's for customer support, personal assistance, or entertainment, your agent will be ready to interact with users in meaningful ways.

Chapter 5: Integrating AI Agents into Applications

5.1 Connecting LM Studio with APIs

API Integration Basics

Once you've developed your AI agent in LM Studio, you'll likely want to integrate it with other applications or services. APIs (Application Programming Interfaces) provide a way for different systems to communicate with each other. In this section, we'll explore how to connect your AI agent to external APIs, which will allow it to access external data, perform tasks, and interact with third-party services.

- **What is an API?**

  An API allows one software application to communicate with another, sending requests and receiving responses in a standardized format. APIs are widely used to connect web applications with databases, payment systems, weather services, social media platforms, and more.

- **Types of API Integrations**
  - **REST APIs**: These are commonly used for web applications. They use HTTP requests (GET, POST, PUT, DELETE) to interact with a remote server and exchange data in JSON or XML format.

- ○ **SOAP APIs**: These are used for more complex transactions. They rely on XML-based messaging and are typically used in enterprise-level integrations.
- ○ **GraphQL**: A flexible API that allows clients to request exactly the data they need. It's often used for more complex querying and retrieving data.

Using Python and JavaScript for Interaction

LM Studio supports several programming languages for API interactions, but Python and JavaScript are among the most commonly used for this task. Here's how you can use these languages to integrate your AI agent with an API:

1. **Python for API Interaction**

    Python is widely used for backend tasks and interacting with APIs due to its simplicity and extensive libraries. The `requests` library is one of the most popular tools for making HTTP requests in Python. Here's a basic example of how to call an API and integrate the response into your AI agent:

```
2. import requests
3.
4. def call_api(endpoint, params):
5.     response = requests.get(endpoint,
   params=params)
6.     if response.status_code == 200:
7.         return response.json()
```

```
8.      else:
9.          return None
10.
11.     api_data =
    call_api("https://api.example.com/data",
    {"query": "weather"})
12.     print(api_data)
```

In this example, the AI agent can use the retrieved data to generate more relevant responses, such as giving weather updates.

13. **JavaScript for Web-Based APIs**
JavaScript is commonly used for web-based applications, and if you're integrating your AI agent into a web interface, JavaScript will be your go-to choice. You can use `fetch` or `axios` to make API calls:

```
14.     function callApi(endpoint, params) {
15.         fetch(endpoint + "?query=" +
    params.query)
16.             .then(response => response.json())
17.             .then(data => {
18.                 console.log(data);
19.                 // Integrate with AI agent
    logic
20.             })
21.             .catch(error =>
    console.error("Error:", error));
22.     }
23.
24.     callApi("https://api.example.com/data", {
    query: "news" });
```

This JavaScript code can be embedded into your web application to pull data from an external API and feed it into the AI agent's responses.

5.2 Building a Chatbot with LM Studio

Frameworks for Chatbot Development

One of the most popular applications of AI agents is in the development of chatbots. Chatbots can handle a variety of tasks, from customer service to entertainment. To create a fully functional chatbot using LM Studio, you need to leverage specific frameworks and tools that integrate seamlessly with LM Studio's capabilities.

- **Rasa**: An open-source framework for building conversational AI, Rasa can be used in combination with LM Studio to create sophisticated chatbots with natural language understanding (NLU). It allows for easy customization and integration with other systems.
- **Botpress**: Another powerful open-source chatbot framework that integrates well with AI models. Botpress provides pre-built modules to handle conversations, intents, and dialogue flows, which can be customized with your trained AI models from LM Studio.
- **Dialogflow**: If you prefer a cloud-based solution, Dialogflow is a good choice for building chatbots. It can be easily integrated with LM Studio via APIs, allowing your local AI models to handle conversation flow while utilizing Dialogflow's user interface.

Example Code Snippets for Chatbot Integration

Here's an example of how to integrate LM Studio into a basic Python-based chatbot:

```python
import openai   # Assuming LM Studio API has a
similar setup
import json

# Initialize the model (example using OpenAI API,
adjust as necessary for LM Studio)
openai.api_key = "your-api-key"

def chatbot_response(user_input):
    prompt = f"User: {user_input}\nAI Agent:"

    # Send request to LM Studio model
    response = openai.Completion.create(
        engine="your-model-id",  # Specify the LM
Studio model you're using
        prompt=prompt,
        max_tokens=150
    )

    # Extract response text
    return response.choices[0].text.strip()

# Example conversation
user_input = "Hello, what can I do today?"
response = chatbot_response(user_input)
print(response)
```

This simple script sends user input to an LM Studio-based model and retrieves a response. You can expand this code to handle more complex conversation flows, manage multi-turn dialogues, and even integrate APIs for additional functionality.

5.3 Enhancing Functionality with Plugins and Extensions

Adding Voice Support

Voice-based interactions are becoming increasingly popular for AI agents, and adding voice support to your chatbot can make the experience more engaging and accessible. Here's how you can integrate voice capabilities into your AI agent:

- **Speech-to-Text (STT)**: Use speech recognition libraries to convert voice inputs into text. Popular libraries include:
  - **Google Speech-to-Text**: A cloud-based solution that offers high accuracy and supports multiple languages.
  - **SpeechRecognition (Python)**: An open-source library that allows you to integrate local speech-to-text capabilities.

  Example of integrating Google Speech-to-Text with Python:

```python
import speech_recognition as sr

recognizer = sr.Recognizer()

def get_audio_input():
    with sr.Microphone() as source:
        print("Listening...")
        audio = recognizer.listen(source)
        try:
```

```
        text                          =
recognizer.recognize_google(audio)
        print(f"You said: {text}")
        return text
    except sr.UnknownValueError:
        print("Could    not    understand
audio.")
        return ""
    except sr.RequestError:
        print("Could not request results
from Google Speech-to-Text.")
        return ""

user_input = get_audio_input()
```

- **Text-to-Speech (TTS)**: Use text-to-speech libraries to convert the AI agent's responses into voice. Popular options include:
  - **Google Text-to-Speech (gTTS)**: A simple Python library to convert text into speech.
  - **pyttsx3**: A Python library that works offline and supports multiple speech engines.

Example of using pyttsx3 to convert the agent's response into speech:

```
import pyttsx3

def speak_response(response):
    engine = pyttsx3.init()
    engine.say(response)
    engine.runAndWait()

speak_response("Hello! How can I assist you
today?")
```

Connecting with Databases and Automation Tools

To enhance your AI agent's functionality, you can connect it to databases and automation tools to retrieve or store data and perform tasks autonomously.

- **Database Integration**: Connect your AI agent to databases like MySQL, PostgreSQL, or NoSQL databases such as MongoDB. This will allow your agent to fetch information, store user preferences, or track interaction history.

  Example of connecting to a MySQL database in Python:

  ```python
  import mysql.connector

  def fetch_user_data(user_id):
      conn = mysql.connector.connect(host="localhost", user="root", password="password", database="user_data")
      cursor = conn.cursor()
      cursor.execute(f"SELECT * FROM users WHERE id = {user_id}")
      result = cursor.fetchone()
      conn.close()
      return result
  ```

- **Automation Tools**: Integrating your AI agent with tools like **Zapier** or **IFTTT** allows it to perform automated tasks such as sending emails, posting to social media, or interacting with other apps based on triggers.

By integrating LM Studio-based AI agents with APIs, voice capabilities, databases, and automation tools, you can create a highly functional and versatile agent that offers dynamic, personalized user experiences and automates complex workflows. This chapter has covered the essential techniques for connecting your AI agent to external systems and extending its functionality through plugins and extensions.

Chapter 6: Optimizing and Troubleshooting

6.1 Performance Optimization

Reducing Latency and Improving Response Times

As you develop AI agents locally using LM Studio, optimizing performance becomes crucial, especially when handling large models or complex queries. Latency and slow response times can hinder the user experience, making it important to fine-tune the performance of your agent. Here are a few strategies to improve response times:

- **Model Pruning**: One of the most effective methods for reducing latency is to prune the AI model. This involves removing unnecessary or less important parts of the model while maintaining its functionality. It helps in reducing the computation load, especially for models that are large or have millions of parameters.
- **Batch Processing**: For agents that need to process multiple requests, batch processing can help reduce latency by grouping requests and processing them in parallel, rather than sequentially. This technique is especially helpful when dealing with high-volume queries.
- **Caching Responses**: Implementing caching mechanisms can drastically reduce the time required for generating responses. If an agent frequently receives similar queries, caching allows

the agent to return a precomputed answer, bypassing the need for model inference.

- **Async Programming**: In some use cases, using asynchronous programming (with `asyncio` in Python, for example) can help you process multiple requests concurrently without blocking other processes. This is particularly helpful in chatbot and API integrations where multiple tasks may be happening at once.

Using GPU Acceleration

LM Studio offers the ability to leverage GPU acceleration, which can significantly boost performance, especially for larger models and real-time inference. GPUs are specifically designed for parallel processing and are highly efficient for machine learning tasks.

- **GPU Setup**: Ensure that you have a compatible GPU installed and that it's properly set up. Most machine learning libraries, including LM Studio, use CUDA (NVIDIA's parallel computing platform) for GPU acceleration. Make sure the necessary CUDA libraries are installed on your system for optimal performance.
- **TensorRT for Optimization**: If you're using large deep learning models, NVIDIA's TensorRT library can be employed to further optimize model inference. TensorRT performs model optimizations such as precision reduction and layer fusion, reducing inference time.

- **Optimized Libraries**: Use optimized machine learning libraries like **cuDNN** (CUDA Deep Neural Network library) and **TensorFlow with GPU support** for high-performance execution.

Here's an example of using a GPU-accelerated setup in Python:

```python
import tensorflow as tf

# Check if GPU is available
if tf.config.list_physical_devices('GPU'):
    print("GPU is available")
    device = '/GPU:0'  # Use the first GPU
else:
    print("GPU is not available, defaulting to CPU")
    device = '/CPU:0'

# Model inference with GPU
with tf.device(device):
    model                                    =
tf.keras.models.load_model('your_model_path')
    prediction = model.predict(input_data)
```

6.2 Common Issues and Fixes

Model Loading Errors

Loading models in LM Studio may sometimes result in errors, especially if the models are large or have specific dependency requirements. Common issues and fixes include:

- **Incorrect File Paths**: Ensure that the file path to the model is correct and that the file is not corrupted. Double-check that the model file is in the correct format (e.g., `.bin`, `.h5`, or `.pt`).
- **Insufficient Memory**: Loading large models requires a significant amount of system memory (RAM). If the system runs out of memory, you may encounter errors. Reducing model size (via quantization or pruning) or increasing the available RAM can resolve these issues.
- **Mismatched Model Version**: Ensure that the model you're trying to load is compatible with the version of LM Studio you're using. Some older models may not be compatible with newer LM Studio versions due to updates in the underlying framework.

  Fix: Use the appropriate model version or update LM Studio and the model to their latest versions for compatibility.

Memory and Performance Troubleshooting

- **Memory Leaks**: When running large models or training locally, memory leaks can occur, especially if certain objects or variables are not properly cleared from memory. These memory leaks can lead to performance degradation over time.

Fix: Use memory profiling tools to identify memory leaks. In Python, libraries such as `memory_profiler` and `tracemalloc` can help track memory usage.

- **Swapping to Disk**: When the system runs out of RAM, it may begin swapping to disk, which significantly reduces performance. Ensure your system has enough RAM for the tasks you're running or reduce the batch sizes to fit within the available memory.

  Fix: Consider adding more RAM to your machine if necessary or optimizing your code to reduce memory consumption (e.g., processing data in smaller chunks).

Compatibility Issues

- **Library Conflicts**: If you are using multiple machine learning libraries (e.g., TensorFlow, PyTorch, and LM Studio), there could be conflicts between them, leading to errors or slow performance.

  Fix: Use virtual environments to isolate the dependencies for each project. This ensures that the correct versions of libraries are used without interference.

- **Outdated Drivers**: GPU-accelerated tasks often require up-to-date drivers for optimal performance. Running outdated GPU drivers may result in reduced performance or errors during model inference.

Fix: Always check for the latest GPU drivers and CUDA toolkit updates from NVIDIA or your hardware provider.

6.3 Best Practices for Running AI Locally

Security Considerations

When running AI models locally, security is an essential aspect to consider, particularly for sensitive applications such as healthcare or finance.

- **Local Hosting**: By running AI models locally, you reduce the risk of data leakage or unauthorized access since there is no need to send sensitive data to the cloud. However, you still need to secure the local environment.
- **Access Control**: Ensure that only authorized users can access the local AI environment by implementing access control mechanisms. Use strong passwords, multi-factor authentication, and network security measures such as firewalls.
- **Model Integrity**: Make sure the models you are using are verified and come from trusted sources. Malicious actors could compromise models to introduce vulnerabilities.

Data Privacy Measures

- **Data Anonymization**: If you're processing sensitive or personal data, ensure that the data is anonymized before being used in training or inference. This prevents privacy violations and ensures compliance with data protection regulations (e.g., GDPR, CCPA).
- **Encryption**: Encrypt sensitive data both at rest (when stored) and in transit (when being processed or transferred). This ensures that even if unauthorized access occurs, the data remains secure.
- **Data Storage**: When storing data locally, consider using encrypted storage systems to further protect sensitive information.

Keeping Models Updated

AI models are constantly evolving, and newer versions often come with improved accuracy, efficiency, and security. Keeping your models up-to-date ensures that your AI agent benefits from the latest advancements in technology.

- **Model Updates**: Regularly check for updates or new versions of the models you're using. Some model providers offer automated update features, or you can subscribe to mailing lists or repositories that notify you of updates.
- **Training New Models**: Over time, the data you use to train your AI agent might become outdated. Re-training models with the latest data or fine-tuning

them on new datasets can help improve their accuracy and relevance.

- **Monitor Model Performance**: Even after deployment, continuously monitor the performance of your model. If it begins to degrade or show signs of bias or drift, it may need to be retrained or adjusted.

This chapter has covered essential strategies for optimizing the performance of your AI agent, troubleshooting common issues, and adhering to best practices for security and model maintenance. By following these guidelines, you can ensure that your AI agents remain reliable, efficient, and secure in a local environment.

Chapter 7: Future of Local AI Agents

7.1 Emerging Trends in Local AI Development

Advances in Lightweight Models

As AI development progresses, one of the most exciting trends is the advancement of **lightweight models**. These models aim to provide the same high-quality results as their larger counterparts but with significantly reduced computational requirements. This trend is especially beneficial for local AI agents, as it allows them to run efficiently on devices with limited resources, such as personal computers, edge devices, and even smartphones.

- **Smaller, Faster Models**: The demand for **low-latency** and **resource-efficient** AI applications has driven the development of smaller models that can be run locally without sacrificing too much performance. Techniques like **knowledge distillation**, where a larger, more complex model teaches a smaller model to mimic its behavior, are becoming more popular. These lightweight models are easier to deploy on local hardware while still delivering impressive results.

- **Quantization and Pruning**: To further reduce the size of models, techniques like **quantization** (reducing the precision of the model's weights) and **pruning** (removing unimportant neurons or weights) are being integrated into model architectures. These techniques allow for faster inference and lower resource consumption while maintaining a high level of accuracy.

- **Optimized Hardware Support**: The growing support for specialized hardware, such as **ASICs** (Application-Specific Integrated Circuits) and **FPGAs** (Field-Programmable Gate Arrays), is also contributing to the development of more efficient models. These chips are optimized for specific AI tasks and are increasingly being integrated into edge devices, allowing for high-performance AI applications even in low-power environments.

In the near future, expect AI models to become more modular and optimized for running locally, providing more opportunities for real-time, context-aware applications across various industries.

Future Improvements in LM Studio

LM Studio itself is poised for significant advancements as the AI landscape continues to evolve. Some of the future developments to look out for include:

- **Enhanced Model Support**: As more models are developed and released by the AI community, LM Studio will likely expand its support to include cutting-edge architectures, ensuring that users can work with the most advanced models available.
- **Seamless Integration with New Hardware**: LM Studio will likely improve its integration with specialized hardware, allowing users to run models

on devices such as GPUs, TPUs (Tensor Processing Units), and other AI-optimized hardware. This will make it easier for users to take full advantage of their local infrastructure and achieve optimal performance.

- **Better User Interface (UI) and UX**: As the demand for AI solutions grows, LM Studio will continue to refine its user interface, making it more intuitive and accessible for both beginners and advanced users. Expect more streamlined workflows, enhanced debugging tools, and a greater emphasis on ease of use.
- **Collaborative Development Features**: With AI development becoming more collaborative, LM Studio may introduce new features that allow multiple users to work on a project simultaneously. This could involve shared workspaces, version control, and cloud synchronization for teams developing AI agents locally.

7.2 Expanding AI Agent Capabilities

Multimodal AI (Text, Image, Audio Processing)

One of the most exciting directions for local AI agents is **multimodal AI**—the ability to process and understand multiple types of data, such as **text**, **images**, and **audio**, all within the same model. Multimodal models allow AI agents to perform more complex and versatile tasks, such as analyzing text and images together for context or responding to voice commands.

- **Text and Image Integration**: Local AI agents will increasingly be able to combine text-based data with visual inputs, enabling applications such as real-time image captioning, video content analysis, and even AI-driven design tools that use both image recognition and text processing to generate content.
- **Audio and Speech Processing**: The integration of **speech recognition** and **natural language processing (NLP)** will allow AI agents to comprehend and interact with voice commands. This opens up a wide range of possibilities for voice-driven assistants, personal AI companions, and accessibility tools for those with disabilities.
- **Cross-Modal Understanding**: Advanced multimodal AI systems will be able to combine inputs from various modes, such as combining voice commands with visual context (e.g., asking an AI to identify an object in a video or respond based on both a visual and verbal cue). This creates an entirely new dimension for local AI agents, making them more interactive, intuitive, and human-like.

In the future, we can expect AI agents to seamlessly switch between modalities and combine them in meaningful ways, providing an enriched experience across a variety of devices, from smartphones to wearables to smart home systems.

Local AI in Edge Computing and IoT

The concept of **edge computing** refers to processing data closer to where it is generated, rather than relying on distant cloud servers. This is becoming increasingly important as the number of connected **Internet of Things (IoT)** devices grows. Local AI agents are uniquely positioned to thrive in this environment.

- **IoT-Enabled Smart Devices**: As more devices become "smart" (e.g., smart thermostats, cameras, wearables), there is a growing need for local AI agents that can process data on-site. These agents can make decisions based on real-time data, such as adjusting settings on a smart thermostat based on user behavior or performing immediate diagnostics on a wearable device.
- **Real-Time Decision Making**: Edge devices, equipped with local AI agents, can make faster decisions because they are not reliant on cloud processing. This is crucial for applications where real-time responses are essential, such as autonomous vehicles, industrial automation, or healthcare monitoring.
- **Privacy and Security**: One of the main advantages of local AI in IoT and edge computing is **data privacy**. By processing data on-device, users retain control over their information, reducing the risk of sensitive data being exposed to third-party services. This is particularly important in industries such as

healthcare and finance, where data security is paramount.

- **Autonomous Edge AI Agents**: In the future, AI agents deployed at the edge may become more autonomous, with the ability to learn and adapt locally without the need for constant updates from the cloud. These agents will continually refine their performance, making them highly adaptable to dynamic environments.
- **Network Efficiency**: Local AI agents also reduce the need for constant data transmission to the cloud, saving on bandwidth and reducing latency. This can help alleviate the pressure on network infrastructure, especially in remote or low-bandwidth areas.

The future of local AI agents is full of promise. With advances in lightweight models, enhanced hardware support, and multimodal capabilities, the next generation of AI agents will be more capable, efficient, and integrated into our daily lives. Whether deployed in smart devices, edge computing applications, or personalized assistants, local AI agents are set to revolutionize how we interact with technology. By staying ahead of emerging trends and continuing to innovate, LM Studio and other local AI development platforms will be at the forefront of this exciting transformation.

Conclusion

Recap of Key Takeaways

In this guide, we've explored the powerful capabilities of **LM Studio** and its potential to revolutionize AI agent development locally. From understanding the basics of LM Studio to setting up your environment, selecting and downloading models, and fine-tuning them for your specific needs, we've covered every step of the journey.

Key takeaways include:

- **LM Studio** offers a comprehensive, user-friendly platform for creating AI agents locally, ensuring data privacy, security, and greater flexibility.
- Running AI models **locally** provides enhanced control over performance, reduces reliance on cloud services, and promotes privacy.
- The **customization** options within LM Studio, such as selecting models, fine-tuning them with local datasets, and implementing unique behaviors, allow you to create highly personalized AI agents.
- **Integrating** AI agents into applications, whether through APIs, chatbots, or plugins, unlocks a wealth of possibilities across various industries.
- Finally, optimizing performance and troubleshooting common issues ensures that your AI agent runs efficiently, even as you scale its capabilities.

By mastering LM Studio, you are equipped to take your AI agent development to the next level.

Encouragement to Experiment with LM Studio

Now that you've learned about LM Studio's features and functionalities, it's time to experiment and put your knowledge into practice. Don't be afraid to explore different **models**, **use cases**, and **integrations** to push the boundaries of what's possible with local AI agents. The best way to truly understand LM Studio's potential is by actively building, testing, and refining your AI agents.

Whether you are working on a **chatbot**, a **personal assistant**, or a more complex application, the flexibility of LM Studio allows you to continuously iterate, optimize, and innovate. The more you experiment, the more you'll uncover hidden possibilities and techniques that will shape your approach to AI development.

Remember, the world of AI is constantly evolving, and by getting hands-on with LM Studio, you'll stay at the cutting edge of local AI technology.

Further Resources for Learning and Community Support

As you continue your journey with LM Studio and local AI development, there are plenty of **resources** and **communities** to help you along the way:

- **Official LM Studio Documentation**: Visit the official LM Studio website for in-depth documentation, tutorials, and FAQs. This is an excellent starting point for troubleshooting and discovering new features.
- **Online Forums and Communities**: Platforms like **Stack Overflow**, **Reddit**, and the **LM Studio user forums** offer opportunities to ask questions, share your projects, and connect with other developers. Join discussions to exchange tips and solutions with a global community.
- **AI Development Courses and Webinars**: Explore online courses on platforms like **Coursera**, **Udemy**, and **edX** to deepen your understanding of AI development, machine learning, and model optimization. Some courses even focus specifically on local AI agents and tools like LM Studio.
- **GitHub Repositories**: Many developers share their LM Studio-related projects on **GitHub**, offering open-source code, collaboration opportunities, and inspiration for your own work.
- **YouTube Channels**: Check out tutorials and walkthroughs on YouTube, where AI enthusiasts and experts share practical guides and real-world examples of building AI agents with LM Studio.

With these resources at your fingertips, you'll always have support as you continue to explore the exciting possibilities of local AI agent development.

By diving into LM Studio, you are opening up a world of potential for creating powerful, efficient, and secure AI agents. The future of AI is local, and you are now equipped to be part of that transformation! Happy experimenting and building!

www.ingramcontent.com/pod-product-compliance
Lightning Source LLC
La Vergne TN
LVHW051618050326
832903LV00033B/4555